My Best Book of
Snakes

Christiane Gunzi

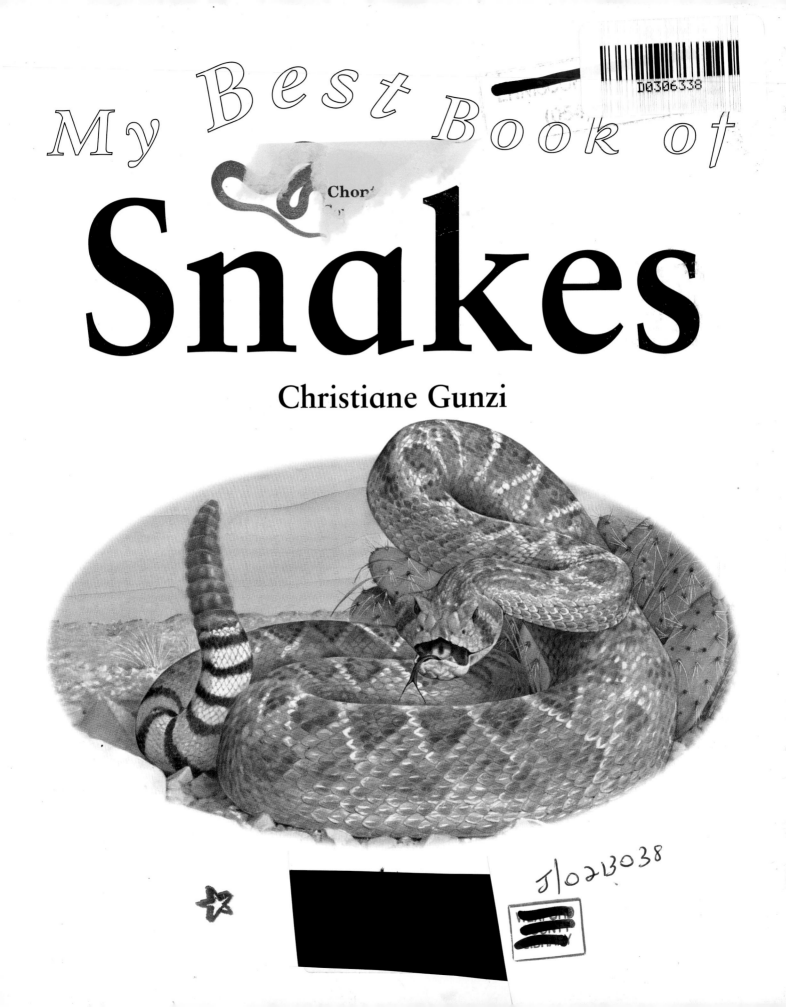

Contents

KINGFISHER

Kingfisher Publications Plc,
New Penderel House,
283–288 High Holborn,
London WC1V 7HZ

www.kingfisherpub.com

Created for Kingfisher by
Picthall & Gunzi Limited

Author and editor: Christiane Gunzi
Designer: Dominic Zwemmer

Illustrator: Michael Langham Rowe

Additional illustrations: Ian Jackson,
David Marshall, Phil Weare,
David Wright

Consultant: Mark O'Shea

KINGFISHER
Kingfisher Publications Plc,
New Penderel House,
283–288 High Holborn
London WC1V 7HZ

www.kingfisherpub.com

First published by Kingfisher
Publications Plc 2003

10 9 8 7 6 5 4 3 2 1

1TR/0603/WKT/MA(MA)/128/KMA

A CIP catalogue record for this book
is available from the British Library.

ISBN 0 7534 0822 8

Printed in China

Meet the snake

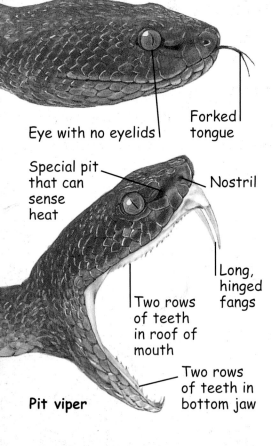

Snakes are amazing animals. **They have no legs, but can crawl, swim, and climb well.**

All snakes hunt their prey, and they always swallow it whole. Some snakes, such as vipers, use venom (poison) to kill prey, while pythons squeeze victims to death. All snakes are covered in scaly skin, and they slough (shed their skin) several times a year. Several species are very venomous and extremely dangerous as well. But most snakes are completely harmless!

Eye with no eyelids

Forked tongue

Special pit that can sense heat

Nostril

Long, hinged fangs

Two rows of teeth in roof of mouth

Two rows of teeth in bottom jaw

Pit viper

A snake's body

A snake is covered with scales. Its forked tongue flicks in and out to pick up smells in the air. Some snakes, such as this viper, have 'pits' on the face to help them find warm-blooded prey.

Slim, muscular body

Strong, scaly skin

No ears and no hearing

Sensitive tongue

Prehensile tail to help with climbing

Nocturnal snakes have vertical pupils, like a cat's.

White-lipped pit viper

4

Power of the python

The reticulated python is a powerful predator. It is not venomous, but it is so strong that it can overpower and eat large mammals. During the day, this handsome snake likes to sleep and rest in trees in the sun.

A leopard is a predator, but it can also be prey for a python.

A world of snakes

Snakes have existed for millions of years. There are about 2,800 different kinds, and most of them are harmless. Snakes belong to several groups, such as the python, cobra and viper families. These cold-blooded animals are reptiles, so they need the heat of the sun to warm them. Most snakes live in the warmest parts of the world. The world's most venomous snakes are found in Africa and Australia.

Boa constrictor
(Central and South America)
2–4m long

Asian sunbeam snake
(Southeast Asia)
1–1.3m long

Green anaconda
(South America)
6–8m long

Western coralsnake
(USA and Mexico)
40–55cm long

Gaboon viper
(Africa)
1.2–2m long

Champion constrictors

The green anaconda is the largest and heaviest snake and the reticulated python is the longest. Both of these beautifully patterned creatures live in the tropics, close to water. They are both 'constrictors', so they kill their prey by squeezing it until it suffocates.

Brahminy blindsnake
(Worldwide)
15–18cm long

Reticulated python
(Southeast Asia)
6–10m long

6

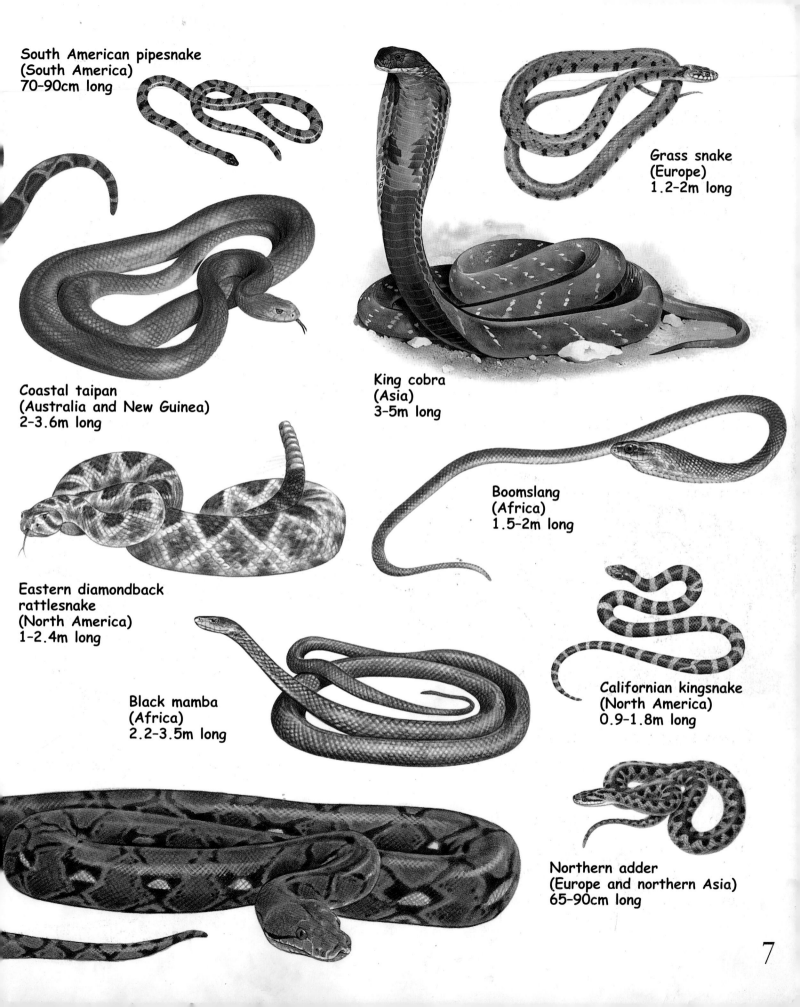

South American pipesnake
(South America)
70-90cm long

Grass snake
(Europe)
1.2-2m long

Coastal taipan
(Australia and New Guinea)
2-3.6m long

King cobra
(Asia)
3-5m long

Eastern diamondback
rattlesnake
(North America)
1-2.4m long

Boomslang
(Africa)
1.5-2m long

Black mamba
(Africa)
2.2-3.5m long

Californian kingsnake
(North America)
0.9-1.8m long

Northern adder
(Europe and northern Asia)
65-90cm long

7

Sidewinding over the sand

When a desert snake has to travel over loose, hot sand, it keeps most of its belly off the ground by throwing its body forward in a series of loops. Only a small part of the snake's body touches the ground at a time. This movement is called 'sidewinding', and snakes that do this are known as sidewinders.

Sidewinding adder in the Namib desert

Eyes are on top of the head so the adder can see prey when the rest of its body is hidden in sand.

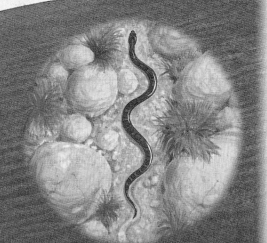

Cornsnake

Serpentining snakes

Long, slim snakes serpentine by moving their body in a series of 'S'-shaped curves while they push against any little bumps on the ground.

Anaconda

Caterpillar crawling

Big, heavy snakes, such as pythons and boas, creep along in a straight line a bit like a caterpillar. Snakes use special scales on their bellies to grip the ground.

How snakes move

Snakes have several kinds of movement. The most common is a method called 'serpentining'. There are powerful muscles inside a snake's body. These muscles produce a series of waves that travel along the snake's body, from its head to its tail. Some snakes, such as black mambas, can move very fast in short bursts. But most snakes do not move quickly unless they are being threatened.

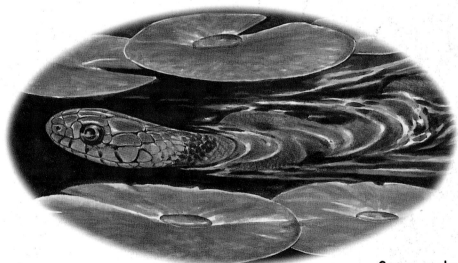

Grass snake

Taking a dip

A grass snake often swims along rivers with its head out of the water, searching for frogs and fish. These reptiles move well on land, and are also found in woodlands and marshes. Grass snakes are completely harmless to humans. If one is caught it usually pretends to be dead!

Baby snakes

Some snakes, such as vipers and boas, give birth to live young. Others, such as cobras and pythons, lay eggs. Snakes that give birth to live young have the most babies. Egg-laying snakes like to lay their eggs in warm, damp places. Unlike the hard shells of bird and turtle eggs, snake eggs are leathery. Once the young are born or hatch from their eggs, they are left on their own by their mother.

Rattlesnake males wrestling for a mate

Snake wrestling

Some male snakes have a wrestling match to decide which one will mate with the female. They lift up the front of their bodies and push each other around!

Carpet python and eggs

Shaking snake

A female carpet python lays 12 to 54 eggs. Unlike other egg-laying snakes, which lay their eggs then abandon them, pythons coil around the eggs to keep them warm. The mother snake shudders every so often, and this may help her eggs to develop.

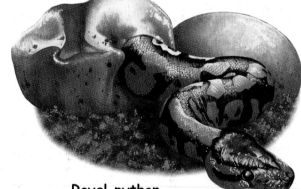

Royal python hatching from its egg

Hatching out

A baby snake cuts its way out of its shell using a sharp 'egg tooth' at the front of its mouth. The egg collapses once the snake has hatched.

10

Stunning stripes

The San Francisco garter snake is one of the most attractive snakes in the world. During the summer, female garter snakes give birth to 12 to 50 live young. This snake lives close to water in meadows, marshes and damp woodlands in California, USA. It is an endangered species because its natural habitat is under threat.

San Francisco
garter snake
with newborn young

Hunting and feeding

Snakes are carnivores, and they eat other animals. Some snakes kill prey with venom, so they are known as 'venomous'. Others kill prey by squeezing, or constricting it. These snakes are called 'constrictors'. All snakes have special lower jaws which can expand, making their mouths open very wide. This means that snakes can eat animals that are much larger than they are!

Copperhead

Fierce fangs

Venomous snakes inject prey with poisonous venom through sharp, pointed teeth called fangs. The venom kills the prey very quickly.

Catching a caiman

The biggest snakes, such as pythons and anacondas, can overpower animals as large as crocodiles. The massive green anaconda spends much of its life in the rivers of South America, where it ambushes deer, jaguars and caimans. It could even eat a human!

A snake that swallows eggs

 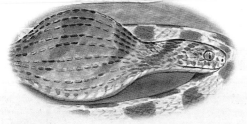 

1 The toothless egg-eating snake eats birds' eggs. It holds the egg in place with its body, then swallows it.

2 As the snake swallows the egg, lots of sharp 'spurs' in its throat puncture the egg so that it breaks.

3 The contents of the egg go into the snake's stomach, and after a while the eggshell is regurgitated.

Green anaconda constricting a spectacled caiman

13

Warning signals

The venom from the fangs of a venomous snake is so deadly that many people are afraid of snakes. But a snake only attacks when it is alarmed, hungry, or feels threatened. It will usually give a warning signal before it strikes. The snake may make a loud noise, lift its head up, or inflate its body to make itself look bigger. All these signals tell its enemies to stay well away!

Rising anger

When a cobra is annoyed, it lifts up the front of its body and spreads out its 'neck hood'. If this warning is ignored, the snake may attack.

A rattlesnake lifts its tail and shakes the 'rattle' loudly.

Huffing and puffing

The puff adder is very dangerous. It is so well camouflaged that it is quite difficult to see. When a puff adder is disturbed, it puffs out its body, hisses loudly, then strikes. Its venom can kill a rat in seconds.

Deadly striker

When a western diamondback rattlesnake is alarmed, it lifts the front of its body into an 'S'-shape and rattles its tail. This warns others to leave it alone. When the snake strikes, it is very quick, and its bite can kill a human.

West African
gaboon viper
in leaf litter

Lethal in the leaves

The gaboon viper is so perfectly disguised that it is almost impossible to see it among the leaves on the forest floor. It hunts by waiting for rats, squirrels and other prey to wander past. Even the top of this snake's head looks like a dead leaf!

Colour and camouflage

 **Snakes have a perfect way of hiding from prey and predators.** The different colours and patterns on a snake's body help to disguise it. This is known as camouflage. Desert snakes are the colour of sand, and forest snakes may be patterned like leaves, so that predators and prey do not see them among the trees. Some snakes, such as coralsnakes, have bright bands of colour that warn enemies to go away.

Looking like a twig

The brown vinesnake is the same shape as the long, thin vines that grow up trees in the forests where it lives. When this snake stays still, it is very difficult to spot.

A friend or foe?

Some harmless snakes look very like venomous snakes. The colours and patterns on a false coralsnake are quite similar to those on a deadly coralsnake. It is important to learn the difference!

Venomous coralsnake

Harmless false coralsnake

King cobra

The world's longest venomous snake is the king cobra. This is the only snake that builds a nest. The female pulls dead leaves into a mound with her body, then makes two underground 'rooms' in it. One room is for her and the other is for her eggs. She lays up to 50 eggs and guards them fiercely. King cobras are extremely venomous, so a female protecting her eggs is very dangerous, even to elephants. She could kill an elephant with one bite to the tip of its trunk!

Guarding the nest

If a king cobra feels threatened by another animal, it growls deeply and shows one of its fangs. It raises the front of its body off the ground and flattens its neck hood, which makes it look bigger. This behaviour warns animals to stay away, or risk being bitten.

Female king cobra fiercely guarding her nest

19

Swamp killer

This big, heavy snake is a kind of pit viper and it has a very venomous bite. The cottonmouth spends much of its life in water, and lives in the swamps, rivers and marshes of the United States. It gets its name because the inside of its mouth is as white as pure cotton. The cottonmouth is not usually aggressive, but when this snake is annoyed, it opens its mouth wide to show its deadly fangs and the pure white lining of its mouth.

A cunning way to catch prey

Cottonmouths are born with bright yellow tails. These newborn snakes have an unusual way of catching the frogs that are their prey – they simply wave the tips of their tails. The frogs mistake the tails for wriggling worms, and then get eaten!

White bite

During the day a cottonmouth basks in the sun on logs and stones at the water's edge. At dawn and dusk it hunts for fish, frogs, lizards, turtles, birds, and other snakes as well. The cottonmouth's only real enemies are king snakes, herons, and humans, of course!

Cottonmouth striking at a green frog

Fast and furious

The black mamba is the longest venomous snake in Africa. Its bite is so deadly that its victims die within an hour of being bitten. Just two drops of venom from this snake's fangs are enough to kill a human. Mambas feed mainly on rodents such as rats. Like other snakes, they can open their mouths very wide and are able to swallow extremely large prey. The black mamba's closest relatives are green mambas. These beautiful snakes are deadly too!

Green mamba
This green mamba spends its life in trees in the forests near the East African coast. Its colour camouflages it so well that other animals do not see the snake in the trees.

The only part of a black mamba that is black is the inside of its mouth.

Menacing mamba

This strong snake can speed along at 23 km/h over short distances. It is very good at climbing as well. A mamba can lift the front of its body one metre off the ground to strike at prey such as rats.

Rats are a black mamba's favourite prey.

Ocean swimmers

Some snakes spend their whole lives in the sea, and they can stay underwater for hours at a time.
These sea snakes have unusual paddle-shaped tails to help them swim. Like other snakes, they shed their skin as they grow. But a sea snake does this more often, possibly to get rid of tiny creatures called parasites on its body. The beaked sea snake is among the most venomous of all animals. One bite contains enough venom to kill 50 people!

A sea snake's cousin
Sea kraits are closely related to sea snakes, but they come on to land to lay their eggs. A true sea snake never goes on land and has live young.

Types of sea snake
There are about 53 different species, or kinds, of sea snake. Most of them live in the ocean and on coral reefs. A few types of sea snake are found in river estuaries and mangrove swamps.

Hardwickes' sea snake

Turtle-headed sea snake

Olive sea snake

Beaked, or common sea snake

Horned sea snake

24

Rubbish collects on the surface where the currents meet, so the fish come here to eat and the sea snakes eat the fish.

A sea snake's nostrils are high on its head, and have valves that open and close for swimming underwater.

Yellow-bellied sea snake

Far out to sea, in the middle of the Pacific Ocean, yellow-bellied sea snakes live in groups of thousands. During the day, they feed near the water's surface. They grab fish, such as mullet and anchovies, that shelter beneath their coils.

Graceful glider

In the lush rainforests of Southeast Asia there are flying snakes. These unusual creatures do not really fly, but they can glide through the air to escape from predators. If a flying snake needs to escape quickly from a bird of prey, it simply leaps into the air and glides safely to the ground. As the snake glides, its ribs expand, so that the underside of the body becomes wide and flat. This is a perfect shape for gliding. The most colourful of these snakes is the beautiful paradise flying snake.

A hawk overhead frightens a group of langur monkeys, and their noise scares the snake away.

Clever climber

The paradise flying snake is an excellent climber, and it can easily travel up the smooth bark of tall, straight trees. This slender snake has special ridges on the scales of its belly that help it to grip as it climbs.

Living on the edge

The broad-headed snake lives under flat sandstone rocks on the edge of cliffs. It is one of the most endangered snakes in Australia. Most of this snake's natural habitat has been covered by the city of Sydney. Sadly, there are not many places for this snake to live in the wild anymore. Many people collect the sandstone under which it lives, and put the rocks in their gardens!

Broad-headed snake in its natural habitat, near Sydney, Australia

Snakes in danger

Like all wild animals, snakes are threatened because their natural habitats, such as rainforests, are being destroyed. Snakes are also in danger from pollution in rivers and seas. But the biggest threat to snakes is from humans. Each year, thousands of snakes are rounded up and slaughtered because people are afraid of them. If we do not protect these beautiful, fascinating animals in the wild, they may become extinct.

Chinese medicines

Snakeskin bag

Road rage

In the desert areas of the world, road surfaces become very hot in the sun. In the evenings, desert snakes often lie on these roads to warm themselves. Many snakes are accidently killed by traffic. Unfortunately, some drivers will run a snake over on purpose, and many of them are killed in this way.

Snakeskin shoes

How snakes are used

In some countries, thousands of wild snakes are killed every year. Their beautiful skin is made into handbags, shoes, wallets and belts for the tourist trade. In some parts of the world, snakes are used in medicines too.

Snakeskin belt

Studying snakes

Snakes have existed for more than 65 million years, and there is still a lot to learn about these amazing animals. Scientists who study snakes are called herpetologists. They look at snakes in their natural habitats to discover exactly how they live. Like all animals, snakes have a role to play in the natural world, and they deserve our respect. You can find out more about snakes by going to see some at a zoo or wildlife park.

Milking snakes

Experts collect venom from the fangs of venomous snakes. This is known as 'milking'. The venom is then made into 'antivenin' to treat people who have been bitten by a venomous snake.

Seeing snakes up close

Reptile keepers often encourage visitors to look at snakes up close. If the keeper allows you to stroke a snake, you will discover that its skin is not slimy or cold, but is dry and warm to touch!

Reptile keeper showing a python to some visitors

Glossary

camouflage The different colours and markings on a snake that help it to hide in the wild.

carnivore An animal, such as a cat, dog or snake, that eats meat.

cold-blooded An animal, such as a reptile, which must bask in the sun to warm its body. It cannot produce its own body heat.

constrictors Snakes such as boas and pythons, which squeeze their victims to death.

egg tooth A temporary tooth that some baby snakes use to cut their way out of their shells.

extinct An animal or plant that has died out forever.

fangs The long, pointed teeth on a venomous snake that inject prey with venom.

habitat An animal's habitat is its natural home in the wild.

hood
The part of a snake's neck that gets wider when the snake, such as a king cobra, feels threatened.

mammals Warm-blooded animals, such as deer, cats and rats, that are covered with fur or hair, give birth to live young and feed them milk.

nocturnal An animal that is active at night. Rat snakes are nocturnal animals.

parasites Tiny creatures that live inside, or on, another animal. Fleas and lice are parasites.

pits The tiny holes on some snakes' faces that help them to sense mammals.

predators Animals that hunt other animals. Snakes are predators.

prehensile tail A tail that can grip. Some snakes that live in trees have prehensile tails for holding on to branches.

prey Animals that are hunted and eaten by snakes and other predators.

reptile Certain cold-blooded animals with scaly or leathery skin, such as snakes, crocodiles, lizards, tortoises and turtles.

sloughing
Shedding the outer layer of skin. Snakes slough their skin every few weeks or months. The skin often comes off in one long piece.

species A group of animals that look alike and are very closely related to each other.

venom A poisonous liquid that venomous snakes inject into their prey when they bite it. Snakes also use venom for self-defence.

venomous Animals that use venom to kill prey. Sea snakes are highly venomous snakes.

warm-blooded An animal, such as a mammal or bird, that produces its own body heat. Mammals can live in cold places.

Index